Rory McIlroy - T
Champion Who Completed
Golf's Grand Slam.

*A Definitive Biography of the Prodigy
from Holywood and His Historic
2025 Augusta Triumph.*

Wilbur I. Boyd

TABLE OF CONTENTS.

INTRODUCTION

The Green Jacket and the Ghosts of Augusta

The sun filtered softly through the Georgia pines as Rory McIlroy stood over his final putt on the 18th green at Augusta National. His posture was still, his breathing measured, his eyes locked on the ball as if nothing else existed. The gallery around him was hushed—an electrified silence that somehow roared in anticipation. Just feet away stood the ghosts of opportunities past: 2011's back-nine collapse, years of frustrating Sundays, whispers of a mental block. But in this moment, it was all behind him. The ball rolled true, dropped into the cup, and with it, so did a decade's worth of weight from McIlroy's shoulders.

It was April 13, 2025, and Rory McIlroy had finally done it. He won the Masters. The only major that had eluded him for over a decade was now his. In doing so, he became just the sixth male golfer in history to complete the modern career Grand Slam—joining the likes of Gene Sarazen, Ben Hogan, Gary Player, Jack Nicklaus, and Tiger Woods. But he was the first European to do it. In a sport so steeped in tradition,

McIlroy had carved his name into history in the most poetic way possible: by exorcising his personal demons on golf's most sacred ground.

The Masters wasn't just the final jewel in Rory's crown. It was his obsession, his white whale. Fans had watched him come close so many times—most painfully in 2011, when he held a four-shot lead heading into the final round, only to unravel spectacularly with an 80. It was a collapse that might've broken lesser players. But McIlroy's career would be defined not just by his wins, but by the resilience that followed that heartbreak. Each year, Augusta reminded him—and the world—of what was missing. Every March, articles recycled the same storyline: "Can McIlroy complete the Slam?" And every April, the answer was: not yet.

That question hung over him longer than anyone expected. He racked up wins elsewhere—two PGA Championships, a U.S. Open, an Open Championship, multiple FedEx Cups—but the Masters became his personal Everest. He finished in the top 10 at Augusta seven times between 2014 and 2023, but always seemed to falter on Saturday or Sunday. There was no technical flaw to point to, no swing deficiency. It was Augusta itself—a course that demands precision and punishes nerves—that repeatedly held him at bay.

And then came 2025.

McIlroy entered the tournament in strong form, having just won the Players Championship in March. But few were willing to make bold predictions. Fans had been burned before. "Augusta's different," pundits said. "You can't predict how Rory will handle Sunday." But this time, the script changed. Despite a shaky start and some tense moments, McIlroy played the weekend with a level of calm rarely seen from him in Georgia. His putter, long the Achilles heel at Augusta, was steady. His iron play was precise. And most importantly, he looked comfortable—at peace with the course and with himself.

The final round was far from a coronation. Justin Rose, playing in the final group, kept the pressure on. When McIlroy bogeyed 18 and Rose birdied 17, the Masters headed to a sudden-death playoff. The tension was unbearable. And then came the moment—McIlroy's approach on the second playoff hole landed within eight feet of the cup. Rose missed his birdie chance, and Rory stepped up for the win.

The putt dropped. He raised both arms, stared at the sky, and then broke down in tears.

The image of McIlroy in a green jacket, smiling through tears, hugging his wife Erica and daughter Poppy, went viral within minutes. It wasn't just a win. It was a moment of catharsis—for Rory, for fans who had followed him for fifteen years, for golf purists who believed in the arc of redemption.

In many ways, McIlroy's Masters win transcends sport. It's a story of patience, maturity, humility, and sheer will. It's about learning to carry expectations—national, personal, and historical—without being crushed by them. It's about evolving, not just as a golfer, but as a human being in the spotlight. McIlroy's journey from boy prodigy in Holywood, Northern Ireland, to global sports icon has always been dramatic. But Augusta gave it its most meaningful chapter.

This book traces that journey in full. From his earliest swings as a toddler guided by his father, to his rise through the amateur ranks, to his global stardom and commercial success, we explore how McIlroy became not just a champion, but one of the defining figures of

21st-century golf. Along the way, we'll revisit his highs—his major wins, Ryder Cup heroics, and clutch victories—and his lows: the collapses, the controversies, and the years where he wondered whether the Slam was out of reach.

But it all leads here—to Augusta. To the Green Jacket. To the moment when talent, perseverance, and timing finally aligned.

Rory McIlroy mastered more than just the course. He mastered the long game—on the course, in his mind, and in life.

Chapter One — Made in Holywood

Before the world knew his name, before the headlines, trophies, and Nike deals, Rory McIlroy was just a wiry kid swinging plastic clubs in a small garden in Holywood, Northern Ireland. The modest seaside town, nestled just outside of Belfast in County Down, was an unlikely incubator for global golfing greatness. Yet it was here, in a working-class home and on local courses etched with wind and grit, that one of the most naturally gifted golfers of all time first learned the rhythm of the game that would define his life.

Rory Daniel McIlroy was born on May 4, 1989, the only child of Gerry McIlroy and Rosaleen "Rosie" McDonald. His parents weren't wealthy, but what they lacked in money, they made up for in drive, sacrifice, and a near-religious belief in their son's potential. His father worked multiple jobs—bartending, cleaning, and working at golf clubs—while his mother took on night shifts at a local factory. Every extra penny went toward Rory's development: better equipment, travel to tournaments, access to coaching. They didn't just support his dream—they built the scaffolding around it.

The legend often begins with the plastic club. Rory was two years old when his father gave it to him. He would fall asleep clutching it, carry it everywhere, even to bed. Soon he was swinging it with uncanny form for a toddler. By age five, he could drive the ball 40 yards. By seven, he was already known around the Holywood Golf Club as a "wee genius." There are VHS tapes from the time—Rory, barely tall enough to see over the ball, with a perfect arc and hip rotation that would make adult pros jealous.

His first coach, Michael Bannon, recognized something special. Bannon would become a long-time fixture in Rory's life, guiding his technique while letting Rory's natural flair take center stage. Where other juniors often got caught in mechanical instruction, McIlroy's game was fluid, instinctive. His swing was poetry, not engineering.

Despite his talent, Rory wasn't raised in a bubble of privilege. He attended St. Patrick's Primary School and later Sullivan Upper School, both in the area. Friends remember a polite, focused boy who kept a low profile in the classroom but transformed into something electric with a golf club. He wasn't brash or boastful. He let his scores do the talking.

His ascent through junior golf was meteoric. He won the Doral Junior Classic in Miami at age 10. By 15, he had shot a 61 at his home club—a course record. At 16, he represented Europe in the Junior Ryder Cup. The trajectory was clear: this wasn't just a kid with potential. This was a generational talent.

Still, Northern Ireland in the 1990s and early 2000s was not the easiest place to nurture global sporting ambition. The country was emerging from decades of sectarian conflict known as The Troubles. Sports were often divided by identity—Catholics played Gaelic football, Protestants played rugby and cricket. Golf was relatively neutral ground, but international opportunity was scarce.

Rory's family saw golf not just as sport but as escape. Escape from limitation, from local expectation, from economic struggle. His father, who had once played to scratch and dreamed of turning pro, saw in Rory the realization of a deferred dream. That legacy shaped Rory's sense of purpose. Even as a teen, he understood that his success would be shared—that it was stitched together by the sacrifices of others.

He turned professional in 2007 at the age of 18, immediately gaining attention for his poise and power. But the roots of his confidence ran deep. McIlroy had already competed against, and beaten, top amateurs from around the world. He wasn't wide-eyed on the tee box—he was ready.

The story of Rory McIlroy's rise can often seem preordained in hindsight. But it wasn't. It was built swing by swing, hour by hour, on damp Northern Irish turf. It was built by a family who risked everything for a dream that, for most, is just that—a dream. It was built in Holywood.

Holywood itself takes pride in its favorite son. Locals recall watching a teenager practice until nightfall, working on his short game in freezing rain. There's a mural of Rory in town now. The golf club has renamed its youth section in his honor. And yet, despite the fame and fortune, Rory has never distanced himself from his hometown. He returns often, donates to local causes, and remains grounded in the values forged during those early years.

This chapter of Rory's life is more than just a prelude. It is the foundation. His effortless power, his focus under pressure, even his emotional responses to loss and victory—they were shaped by the small town where he learned not just how to play, but how to persevere.

McIlroy's story is often framed by his battles on golf's grandest stages—Augusta, St. Andrews, the Ryder Cup. But before all that, there was Holywood. And before the world knew his name, there was a boy with a plastic club, a relentless dream, and a father who never stopped believing.

Chapter Two — A Prodigy in Full Swing

By the time Rory McIlroy stepped onto a professional tee box in 2007, he was already carrying the weight of expectations rarely placed on an 18-year-old. But if pressure made diamonds, McIlroy's swing—fluid, violent, balanced—was the rarest kind. What followed in the next few years wasn't just a rise; it was a signal that golf had entered a new era. He didn't tiptoe into the sport. He kicked the door down.

His amateur career had already turned heads across continents. In 2005, he won both the Irish Close Championship and the West of Ireland Championship, becoming the youngest ever to do so. The same year, he helped Ireland win the European Amateur Team Championship. But it was in 2006 that he gave the golfing world a formal introduction, finishing as the leading amateur at the British Open at Royal Liverpool. His mop of brown curls, his easy swing, and his 291 total—good for tied 42nd—set the media ablaze.

Turning pro in September 2007, McIlroy wasted no time. In his second European Tour event as a professional, the Alfred Dunhill Links Championship, he finished third. A top-200 world ranking within two months. Just a year later, he claimed his first professional win at the 2009 Dubai Desert Classic, birdieing the final hole with icy nerves to edge Justin Rose. It made him the seventh-youngest winner in European Tour history. And it was clear this wasn't luck or hot form—it was the emergence of a generational force.

What set McIlroy apart was not just raw talent but how quickly he adapted to the crucible of elite competition. Most rookies struggle with the travel, the noise, the distractions. Rory seemed to thrive in it. He had the poise of a seasoned veteran and the fire of a teenager with something to prove. And most importantly, he had "the swing"—a natural, powerful, whip-crack motion that was as aesthetically pleasing as it was effective. Analysts compared it to Tiger in his prime, but Rory's mechanics had a distinctive Irish rhythm: a mix of aggression and grace.

The breakthrough in the U.S. came at the Quail Hollow Championship in 2010. At 20 years old, McIlroy shot a final-round 62—yes, 62—with a back-nine of 30 to capture his first PGA Tour title.

Golf writers didn't just praise it—they called it one of the greatest closing rounds in Tour history. He had dismantled a difficult course and a seasoned field with a kind of joyful violence. In that moment, McIlroy wasn't just the future of golf; he was the present.

But it wasn't just his results. It was how he carried himself. McIlroy didn't strut or gloat. He was approachable, honest, refreshingly candid. In an era of media-trained automatons, Rory spoke his mind. He laughed off bad rounds. He talked openly about nerves. He admitted when he got ahead of himself. Fans loved him for it. The press loved him even more. In McIlroy, they saw not just a winner, but a story.

Yet prodigies are always tested. In April 2011, McIlroy had a four-shot lead going into the final round of the Masters. It was supposed to be his coronation. Instead, it became a nightmare. He shot an 80—collapsing with wayward drives, missed putts, and a quadruple-bogey at the 10th. He didn't just lose the tournament. He fell apart on the grandest stage. Critics called it a choke. Pundits speculated whether he could ever recover.

Rory, to his credit, didn't flinch.

He returned just two months later and demolished the field at the U.S. Open at Congressional. He shot a tournament-record 268, finishing at 16-under par. It was dominance, redemption, and a statement rolled into one. He wasn't wounded from Augusta—he was forged by it.

That summer in 2011 marked the full arrival of McIlroy as not just a young winner, but a force capable of changing the sport's landscape. He signed a massive endorsement deal with Nike, moved into the top five of the world rankings, and began building a transatlantic fan base. He wasn't just winning—he was making golf exciting to a new generation.

Critics would say his early stardom came too fast. His personal life, including high-profile relationships and endorsement obligations, sometimes drew more headlines than his play. But Rory always brought it back to the game. Even when he faltered—like his missed cut at the 2013 Open Championship—he spoke openly about needing to grow. He never ducked accountability.

By the end of 2014, he had won four major championships. He was the World No. 1. He was still in his mid-20s.

This chapter in Rory's life wasn't just about success—it was about managing expectations, surviving scrutiny, and learning what it meant to be not just a golfer, but a brand, a public figure, a target. He emerged from it more self-aware, more disciplined, and still swinging with that same explosive beauty that first captured the world's attention.

McIlroy's early years weren't just impressive—they were defining. In a sport known for its slow burns and late bloomers, Rory arrived like a lightning strike. He was a prodigy in full swing, and the world had no choice but to watch.

Chapter Three — Champion by Twenty-Four

By the time Rory McIlroy celebrated his 24th birthday in May 2013, he had already accomplished what most golfers dream of achieving in a lifetime. In just a few years, he had claimed two major championships, reached World No. 1, and firmly established himself as the heir apparent to golf's throne in the post-Tiger era. But behind the glittering success was a young man grappling with the intensity of global stardom, the expectations of a sport hungry for a new icon, and the challenge of managing life in the public eye.

McIlroy's first major title at the 2011 U.S. Open was a thunderous statement. His 16-under-par finish at Congressional not only silenced critics after his Masters collapse earlier that year, but also broke multiple records, including the lowest 72-hole score in U.S. Open history. It was a performance marked by surgical ball-striking and a kind of emotional detachment rare for someone so young. He played like a veteran who had already processed the trauma of losing—because he had.

The victory in 2011 wasn't a fluke. In 2012, McIlroy proved he belonged in the pantheon of golf's greats when he won the PGA Championship at Kiawah Island in a runaway. His margin of victory—eight strokes—was the largest in the tournament's history. The course was brutal, the wind unforgiving, but Rory made it look like a Sunday stroll. With that second major, he reclaimed the world's number one ranking and backed it up by topping both the PGA and European Tour money lists. At 23, McIlroy wasn't just successful—he was dominant.

What made this dominance so compelling was its combination of power and finesse. Rory had one of the longest drives on tour, regularly topping 300 yards, but his precision with irons and silky putting touch made him dangerous from anywhere. He wasn't a one-dimensional bomber. He was complete. And aesthetically, his game was a joy to watch—his swing seemed choreographed by nature itself.

Yet, as 2013 unfolded, the pressures of life at the top began to seep into his game. In January, he signed a blockbuster endorsement deal with Nike reportedly worth over $200 million. The switch brought new clubs, new equipment, and new scrutiny. His performances dipped. A mid-season walk-off at the Honda Classic sparked criticism, as did a public statement about "tooth pain." In the spotlight, everything becomes magnified. For a 23-year-old who had risen too quickly to avoid the hard lessons, it was the beginning of a humbling chapter.

Despite this temporary regression, McIlroy's commitment to learning and growth remained. He began working more closely with his long-time coach Michael Bannon to fine-tune his swing and iron out flaws introduced by the new equipment. He reassessed his approach to fitness, mental preparation, and scheduling. These weren't the moves of a stubborn prodigy—they were signs of maturity. Even in disappointment, Rory was evolving.

Off the course, his relationship with tennis star Caroline Wozniacki drew massive media attention. The public watched as two young, successful athletes navigated a high-profile romance under relentless scrutiny. For Rory, the attention—tabloids, paparazzi, rumors—became part of the balancing act. He wasn't just managing a golf career anymore. He was managing a brand.

Still, the fire burned. McIlroy would close out 2013 with flashes of his former brilliance, but it was in 2014 that everything came roaring back. He began the season with a renewed sense of purpose and a clarity that had been lacking in the previous year. The catalyst may have been his high-profile breakup with Wozniacki in May—just days after their wedding invitations were sent. Rory announced the split publicly and candidly, admitting he wasn't ready for marriage. Some criticized the timing, but he used the emotional turbulence as fuel.

That summer, he went on a historic run. First came victory at the Open Championship at Royal Liverpool—his third major. He led wire-to-wire, holding off surges from Sergio García and Rickie Fowler. His control was absolute. Then, just weeks later, he captured his second PGA Championship at Valhalla in one of the most dramatic finishes in major history. Darkness descended on the course as Rory chased down Fowler and Phil Mickelson, eventually overtaking them with a barrage of fearless shots. He finished the year as World No. 1 again and had four worldwide victories to his name.

By 24, McIlroy was a four-time major winner, a FedEx Cup contender, and a dual-tour money leader. But more importantly, he had shown resilience, self-awareness, and the capacity to adapt under extreme pressure. He wasn't just golf's most talented young player. He was its most introspective. His willingness to take ownership of his struggles—on and off the course—made his comeback more than a sports story. It was human.

In hindsight, McIlroy's early success could've consumed him. Many prodigies lose their way in the transition from youthful potential to adult reality. But Rory charted his course differently. He didn't pretend to have all the answers. He admitted when he was lost. And then, like his swing, he found his center again.

To become a champion is hard. To do it four times before 25—while managing fame, fortune, failure, and growth—is rarer still. Rory McIlroy did not stumble into greatness. He earned it. And he wasn't done.

Chapter Four — Augusta: The Unfinished Symphony

For most golfers, Augusta National is sacred ground. For Rory McIlroy, it became something closer to a haunting. The Masters Tournament, the first major of the year and the most visually iconic, eluded him again and again—not for lack of talent, but because it became the mirror of his career's complexity. While he conquered the other majors before age 26, Augusta stood stubbornly outside his grasp. It was a symphony he could never quite finish, a masterpiece whose final note remained elusive.

The ghosts of Augusta began in earnest in 2011. That year, McIlroy entered Sunday with a four-shot lead, having played three dazzling rounds of golf that showcased the full breadth of his talent. The swing was fluid, the putting confident, the composure mature beyond his years. Through 63 holes, he looked unstoppable.

Then came the collapse.

On the 10th hole—famously difficult even for veterans—McIlroy drove into the trees, hit a branch with his second shot, and triple-bogeyed. The green jacket slipped away in the most painful way: not in a duel, not in defeat by brilliance, but in a slow, public unraveling. He shot an 80. It was one of the most devastating final rounds in Masters history.

Many players might never have recovered. Augusta has a way of turning one mistake into a lifelong wound. But Rory did what great champions do—he came back stronger. Just two months later, he won the U.S. Open at Congressional with a record-setting performance. He had shown resilience. And yet, Augusta still lingered. Each spring, the golf world turned its gaze toward Rory and asked: Is this the year?

Between 2012 and 2024, McIlroy played consistently well at the Masters, often finishing inside the top 10. He had Sunday charges and Thursday sparks, but never quite managed to stitch four elite rounds together. Sometimes it was the putter that failed him. Other times, it was a single bad hole. Augusta doesn't forgive imperfections—it highlights them. And with each passing year, the pressure grew.

The quest for the career grand slam—winning all four majors—only intensified the scrutiny. With wins at the U.S. Open, Open Championship, and PGA Championship already in his cabinet, the Masters was the final piece. Golf history is exclusive: only five male players—Gene Sarazen, Ben Hogan, Gary Player, Jack Nicklaus, and Tiger Woods—had completed the modern Grand Slam. McIlroy stood at the threshold. And the longer he stood there, the heavier the door seemed.

There were moments when it felt within reach. In 2018, he was paired with Patrick Reed in the final group on Sunday, just three shots behind. McIlroy birdied the second hole, and for a moment, the air shifted. But missed putts and mounting pressure derailed the charge. He shot a 74, finishing fifth. In the post-round interview, he was gracious but hollow-eyed. Once again, Augusta had whispered not yet.

Part of McIlroy's struggle with Augusta was psychological. The course doesn't merely test technical skill—it demands emotional mastery. The greens are fast and treacherous, the wind deceptive, the expectations suffocating. And for Rory, each return to Augusta was a return to memory. He wasn't just playing the course—he was playing the ghosts of 2011, the weight of legacy, the echo of every commentator asking if this would finally be the year.

He tried different approaches. In some years, he came in hot from dominant early-season play. In others, he arrived under the radar, hoping lower expectations would free him. He adjusted preparation routines, media strategies, even how he practiced his putting. Nothing worked. The irony was clear: the player with arguably the most natural swing of his generation couldn't solve the puzzle of Augusta.

Through it all, McIlroy evolved. He married, became a father, took leadership roles on the PGA Tour, and became more outspoken about the future of golf. His perspective matured, and with it, a deeper understanding of what Augusta represented. It was no longer about the slam or silencing critics—it was about honoring a lifelong pursuit. Perfection. Mastery. Closure.

The public narrative framed his Augusta story as a failure. But that's too simplistic. Each near-miss was a reminder of how good he was. Most players never come close. Rory kept returning to the brink. His career didn't lack greatness; it lacked a final crescendo.

That is, until 2025.

But before we jump ahead, it's essential to acknowledge what made the wait so significant. The frustration, the anguish, the repeated heartbreak—they're what gave his eventual triumph its meaning. Without the failures, the green jacket would have been just another achievement. With them, it became something else: a resolution, a catharsis, a closing movement to a symphony long in the making.

For years, Augusta was the question mark at the end of Rory McIlroy's resume. Not anymore.

The unfinished symphony had found its final note.

Chapter Five — Peaks, Valleys, and FedEx Fortune

Success in professional golf is rarely linear. For Rory McIlroy, the journey from prodigy to veteran champion has been defined by soaring highs, frustrating lows, and a knack for timing his best golf when it mattered most—especially during the lucrative FedEx Cup Playoffs. If Augusta National tested his emotional endurance, then the PGA Tour's FedEx Cup series became a theater where Rory displayed his resilience, reinvention, and extraordinary staying power.

After bursting onto the major championship scene with his emphatic win at the 2011 U.S. Open, McIlroy followed up with two PGA Championships (2012, 2014) and a Claret Jug (2014). By 25, he had four majors, world number one status, and a swagger that suggested he might dominate the sport for years to come. But then came the valleys—the injuries, the putting woes, the switch in equipment manufacturers, and perhaps most critically, the rise of rivals who caught fire while Rory plateaued.

Between 2015 and 2018, McIlroy endured a stretch of near-misses and growing criticism. He'd win sporadically—sometimes impressively—but questions persisted about his hunger, focus, and whether his best golf was behind him. Some pointed to his intensity fading after the early success, others to external distractions. But what made this period remarkable was that even at "less than his best," McIlroy remained among the most consistent top finishers in the world. His floor was still high.

The FedEx Cup, introduced in 2007, is the PGA Tour's season-long points race culminating in a playoff series with a massive bonus purse. By 2016, McIlroy saw it as more than just money—it was a legacy play, an arena where consistency, resilience, and championship performance all mattered. That year, he put together one of the most thrilling finishes in FedEx Cup history.

At the 2016 Tour Championship, Rory came from behind on Sunday and forced a playoff. He then drained a 15-foot putt for eagle on the 16th hole of the fourth playoff hole to clinch both the Tour Championship and the FedEx Cup title. The emotional outpouring was visible. It wasn't a major, but it felt significant—a validation after a period where the big titles had eluded him. With that win, he joined the select group of players whose games could peak at precisely the right time.

But the path forward remained bumpy. In 2017, injuries and inconsistency crept back in. A nagging rib injury kept him from finding a rhythm, and his winless season further fueled the "Is Rory done?" speculation. It was a familiar cycle: doubt, dismissal, and then resurgence.

The resurgence came again in 2019. That season, McIlroy played some of the most statistically dominant golf of his career, though not in majors. He led the PGA Tour in scoring average, strokes gained off the tee, and strokes gained total—indicators of elite all-around play. He won the RBC Canadian Open, The Players Championship (often dubbed the "fifth major"), and capped it with another Tour Championship victory to claim his second FedEx Cup. In doing so, he became only the second golfer—after Tiger Woods—to win the FedEx Cup twice.

What stood out in 2019 wasn't just the wins—it was the composure. McIlroy had started working more deliberately on the mental aspects of his game, focusing on acceptance, emotional neutrality, and being "process-oriented." He famously adopted a mantra: "Be present." It marked a subtle but powerful shift in his approach. He wasn't chasing validation anymore. He was chasing excellence on his terms.

COVID-19 disrupted the 2020 season, and McIlroy, like many, struggled to find rhythm in the fan-less, uncertain atmosphere. He became a father that year, and while the joy was evident, his game became inconsistent. 2021 and 2022 saw more tinkering—coaching changes, caddie adjustments, and a renewed emphasis on putting.

Then came 2022, a year that reasserted McIlroy's status among golf's elite. In the context of the growing LIV Golf controversy and PGA Tour instability, Rory emerged as the sport's moral compass and its most eloquent spokesman. His performances backed up his words. He won three times, contended in majors, and clinched his third FedEx Cup title—surpassing Tiger Woods.

Winning three FedEx Cups is no small feat. It requires sustained excellence across a full season and the ability to deliver under playoff pressure. For McIlroy, it was also about narrative control. Even without a major since 2014, he had now built a legacy that went beyond the traditional benchmarks. He was a three-time FedEx Cup winner, a four-time major champion, and one of the highest-earning golfers of his generation—not just in prize money, but in prestige.

If Augusta was the white whale, the FedEx Cup was the proving ground. It showcased his ability to rally, to stay relevant, to evolve. Few athletes in any sport can claim both youthful brilliance and mid-career reinvention. McIlroy could.

By the time 2025 rolled around, McIlroy was no longer just the prodigy or the crowd favorite. He was the veteran with scars and stripes. His name had become synonymous with the modern era of golf. Peaks and valleys weren't deviations from his story—they were the story. And in the FedEx Cup, he'd found a recurring platform to remind the world that class, once earned, is never lost.

Next up: Augusta, one more time.

Chapter Six — The Personal Game

Rory McIlroy's greatness has often been measured by statistics—driving distance, major wins, scoring averages. But a fuller portrait of his career emerges when you strip away the leaderboards and swing metrics. What you find is a man whose most profound battles have been inward, whose evolution as a person has directly shaped—and been shaped by—his performance on the course. In the gladiatorial world of professional golf, where pressure isolates and legacy can haunt, Rory's ability to navigate his personal life with grace has been as vital to his success as any technical refinement.

For much of his early twenties, McIlroy was the embodiment of effortless brilliance. With a mop of curls and a grin that never looked forced, he was golf's golden boy. He signed endorsement deals worth tens of millions, played with joyful aggression, and rarely lost the crowd's affection—even when he lost tournaments. But as the victories piled up, so too did the expectations. He became a global figure, a symbol of golf's future, and the demands on his time and psyche grew exponentially.

The first public sign that Rory was struggling to balance the personal with the professional came in 2014, when he ended his engagement to tennis star Caroline Wozniacki just days after wedding invitations had been sent out. It was a raw, very human moment—one he addressed with remarkable honesty. "I wasn't ready for all that marriage entails," he admitted. "The problem is mine." The decision could have become tabloid fodder. Instead, his vulnerability in handling it won many admirers. And, remarkably, he went on to win two majors that summer.

But even as he matured in public, McIlroy continued to wrestle with identity: not just as a golfer, but as a person. He'd grown up in Northern Ireland, a region fraught with political history and tribal allegiances. Rory refused to be a mascot for any one camp. His decision to represent Ireland in the Olympics—after much soul-searching—was both personal and political. In his view, he wanted to honor his roots without being reduced to them. "I play golf," he said. "I'm not a flag."

Off the course, McIlroy sought stability. He found it in Erica Stoll, a former PGA of America employee. They married in 2017 at Ashford Castle in Ireland, far from the media blitz of his early fame. Their relationship marked a turning point: less spectacle, more grounding. Friends noted that Rory became more thoughtful, less reactive. The birth of their daughter Poppy in 2020 deepened that shift. In interviews, he spoke about how fatherhood gave him perspective. "Whether I shoot 65 or 75, she's just happy to see me," he said. It was clear: golf no longer defined his self-worth.

This perspective didn't dull his competitive fire, but it did help him manage the turbulence. For a player so often labeled "streaky," consistency required emotional regulation. McIlroy began working more seriously on his mental game—through meditation, reading, and coaching. He quoted stoic philosophers in pressers. He read Ryan Holiday. He journaled. These weren't gimmicks; they were part of a larger commitment to self-awareness.

His on-course demeanor evolved in parallel. Earlier in his career, he'd let bad holes bleed into bad rounds. But now, there was a steadier calm. At the 2022 Canadian Open, in front of a raucous crowd, McIlroy held off Justin Thomas and Tony Finau in a Sunday shootout. The emotion afterward was raw—he pumped his fist, roared to the crowd, and later revealed that it had meant more than just a win. It was about proving to himself that he still had it.

That same year, McIlroy stepped into an unexpected leadership role as LIV Golf's emergence fractured the sport. He became the de facto spokesperson for the PGA Tour, defending its traditions and values with passion. Whether you agreed with his stance or not, there was no denying his personal growth. He wasn't just playing golf; he was standing for something larger. The burden was heavy, and at times it showed. But McIlroy never ducked the hard conversations.

Privately, those close to him said the pressure was immense—not just from fans or sponsors, but from within. Rory wanted to be more than just a golfer who won young. He wanted to be someone who grew with the game, who left a lasting mark. The chase for the career Grand Slam—a Masters title—was as much about personal closure as professional validation.

When he finally slipped on the green jacket in 2025, the emotion was unmistakable. He hugged Erica and Poppy behind the 18th green. His voice cracked in the Butler Cabin interview. This wasn't just about completing the resume. It was about a man who had weathered fame, failure, expectation, and doubt—and come out whole.

McIlroy's personal game—his marriage, fatherhood, self-examination, moral clarity—has been the unseen caddie guiding his career through its darkest and brightest moments. It didn't win him trophies directly, but it gave him the durability to keep going when trophies stopped coming. And in the long game of legacy, that resilience might be his most lasting achievement.

Chapter Seven — The Players and the Prelude

Before a single shot was struck at the 2025 Masters, the storylines had already been swirling like the unpredictable April winds at Augusta National. This wasn't just another edition of golf's most mythic major. It was a tournament weighed down with expectations, questions, and unresolved rivalries. The field was a rich tapestry of veterans, upstarts, returnees, and controversial figures. But hovering above them all was one persistent narrative: would Rory McIlroy finally win the Masters?

For years, Rory had arrived at Augusta with the same question attached to his name. And for years, the outcome was heartbreakingly consistent—flashes of brilliance undone by a bad round, a cold putter, or the mysterious weight Augusta seemed to place on his shoulders. But 2025 felt different, and not just because of Rory's recent form. The entire competitive landscape had shifted.

Let's begin with the field. By 2025, the PGA Tour and LIV Golf had reached a fragile detente. Some LIV players were back in the majors, injecting tension and intrigue. Jon Rahm, the 2023 Masters champion and one of LIV's high-profile signings, returned to defend his legacy. His game remained ferociously consistent, and his fiery competitiveness made him one of the few players who could stand toe-to-toe with Rory in terms of sheer presence.

Scottie Scheffler, meanwhile, was once again the world number one. With his unflappable demeanor and a short game that bordered on sorcery, he had already picked up two wins early in the season. If Augusta favored calm precision, Scheffler was your man.

Then there was Viktor Hovland—charismatic, clinical, and coming off a quietly dominant winter in Europe. Collin Morikawa had rediscovered his form after a sluggish 2024, and Jordan Spieth, Augusta's prodigal son, remained dangerous no matter his form coming in. There were new faces, too: Ludvig Åberg, now a top-10 mainstay, and a precocious 20-year-old amateur from Japan who had captivated social media with his Tiger-esque shot-making.

The stage was crowded, but Rory's presence loomed largest. He'd won three times already in 2025—in Dubai, at Bay Hill, and at Quail Hollow. But more importantly, he looked like himself again: free-flowing, confident, serene. The media was unusually subdued in the run-up. Maybe out of fatigue. Maybe out of superstition. Still, the subtext was clear—if not now, when?

But Augusta is not won in press conferences. The tournament week began, as always, with the rituals that make the Masters sacred: the Champions Dinner, the Par 3 Contest, the blooming azaleas, and the ceremonial first tee shots. Jack Nicklaus, Gary Player, and Tom Watson opened proceedings with drives that symbolized both history and the ticking clock.

Rory spent much of the practice rounds keeping a low profile. Observers noted he played nine-hole sessions, mostly in the afternoon, staying away from the spotlight and focusing intensely on his putting—long Augusta's undoing. His caddie, Harry Diamond, was unusually chatty with reporters. "He's ready. That's all I'll say. It's different this year," he said, then quickly walked off.

But if Rory was quietly preparing, others were already stirring the pot. Rahm spoke pointedly about "being disrespected" in his absence from PGA events. Brooks

Koepka, still straddling the line between villain and legend, dismissed concerns about LIV players being underprepared: "It's golf, not rocket science." And a viral video of a frosty range encounter between Scheffler and Rahm only stoked the fire.

Narratives began to take shape. Could Rahm defend his green jacket under the microscope? Would Scheffler's machine-like consistency win out over Rory's poetic ambition? Could a dark horse like Hovland or Morikawa take advantage of the distractions? And what of Tiger Woods—still recovering, still revered—who had arrived with little fanfare but endless whispers? He wasn't a contender, but he was a ghost in every corner of the course, a reminder of what greatness looks like in full bloom.

The pairings were announced on Wednesday. Rory would tee off Thursday morning alongside Max Homa and Joaquín Niemann. Not a spotlight group, but not anonymous either. Enough room to breathe. Enough of a reminder that this was business.

And yet, as the sun rose on Thursday, there was a collective tension in the air. Not dread, but anticipation. Golf, like boxing, is a sport defined by rhythm and clash. The prelude was nearly over. The symphony was about to begin.

For McIlroy, the prelude had lasted more than a decade. Each year at Augusta was another verse in a song of what-ifs and almosts. But this year, there was no sense of desperation. Just focus. He seemed lighter—like a man who had already made peace with the course, and with himself.

The players were ready. The field was stacked. The ghosts of Augusta stirred once more. The only thing left was the performance.

Chapter Eight — Sunday at the Masters

The Masters is a tournament where stories are written in every blade of grass and etched into the granite hills of Augusta National. It is the culmination of four days of golf, each more intense than the last. The atmosphere on Sunday at Augusta is unlike anything else in sports—electric, tense, steeped in history, and alive with the sounds of birdies, bogeys, and the sweet hum of anticipation. As Rory McIlroy stepped onto the 1st tee on Sunday of the 2025 Masters, he knew this was not just another round. This was the culmination of a career's worth of expectations, and perhaps, destiny.

For McIlroy, Sunday was special because it was the day he had circled on his calendar for years. It wasn't just a Masters round for him; it was the culmination of a dream—a dream he had come so close to achieving before, only to fall short. The Masters had always been his elusive grand prize, the one major that had slipped from his grasp despite his numerous accolades. But 2025 was different. This time, McIlroy wasn't just competing with the field; he was competing against ghosts—ghosts of past failures, missed opportunities, and the ever-present weight of Augusta's history.

The Setting: The Calm Before the Storm

The weather on Sunday morning was perfect. It was one of those rare, cool, clear days at Augusta—no rain, no wind. The azaleas were in full bloom, their colors sharp against the backdrop of towering pines and the vibrant green fairways. Augusta National looked like it had been plucked straight from a dream, and the patrons were gathered in clusters along the fairways, waiting for the action to begin.

But for McIlroy, it wasn't about the beauty of the course or the crowds. It was about what lay ahead. He had already put himself in the conversation for victory after three rounds, but Sunday was always a different beast. The final round at Augusta could make or break a career. It could elevate a player into the stratosphere of golf legends, or it could expose vulnerabilities that had been concealed for four days.

McIlroy's final pairing was set: he would be playing alongside Jon Rahm, the defending champion, and Scottie Scheffler, the world number one. If anyone knew what it was like to carry the pressure of leading a major, it was these two. Both had been in contention at Augusta before, and both were seasoned enough to handle the massive weight of expectation. But McIlroy had an advantage—the past.

Unlike the others, McIlroy had the ghosts of Augusta etched deeply into his memory. He had felt the heartbreak of coming close in previous years—leading at one point or another, only to falter. But that history had given him the resolve he needed. This was not a man trying to prove himself anymore; this was a man who had already proved his worth.

The Battle Begins: A Strong Start

McIlroy's round began in the calm light of the early morning. His first shot of the day was the embodiment of his growth—solid, confident, and precise. He had learned over the years that the key to Augusta was not just executing under pressure, but embracing the pressure itself. Early on, McIlroy was patient and deliberate, letting the course come to him. His short game, which had been a point of weakness in past Masters, was sharp. His irons, often a cause for concern in earlier rounds, were finding their marks with ease.

But what separated McIlroy from the rest of the field on this Sunday was his mental game. As the holes wore on, it became clear that he was playing with a different kind of intensity. This was no longer just about executing shots—it was about executing under the weight of history. Every putt he sank, every fairway he hit, seemed like a step closer to redemption.

However, it wasn't going to be an easy ride. As McIlroy moved through the course, Rahm and Scheffler were right there with him, pushing the pace. Rahm's fiery competitiveness was evident as he birdied holes 2 and 4, keeping McIlroy on his toes. Scheffler, with his methodical style, wasn't backing down either. But McIlroy matched their efforts with unflinching resolve, birdying the 5th and 8th holes to keep pace with the leaders.

The Turn: Tension Mounts

By the time McIlroy reached the 9th hole, the atmosphere at Augusta was electric. The tension was palpable as the players neared the turn, where the back nine—Augusta's true proving ground—awaited. The famous stretch of holes that includes Amen Corner would be the ultimate test for all three players.

As McIlroy approached the 10th tee, he held a slender one-shot lead over Scheffler and a two-shot advantage over Rahm. The course was playing tricky—slightly faster greens, subtle breezes, and the kind of undulation that Augusta is famous for. The pressure of holding the lead, combined with the knowledge that he had never won here, was immense. But McIlroy was undeterred. He hit a beautiful tee shot on the 10th, followed by a confident second shot to within range of the pin. The eagle putt he sank on the 10th hole—a putt that seemed to freeze time—was the moment the Masters started to feel inevitable.

The Final Push: The Masters in His Grip

With the back nine looming, McIlroy's resolve only strengthened. The ghosts of Augusta, the memories of near misses, the pressure of his own legacy—all of it seemed to fall away. On the 13th hole, after another perfect drive, McIlroy hit an iron to within five feet of the hole, setting up a birdie that pushed his lead further ahead. Rahm and Scheffler were still battling, but McIlroy's play was becoming clinical—relentless.

The 16th hole, as always, proved to be pivotal. With the crowd gathered around the green, McIlroy stood over a 12-foot birdie putt. A putt that, with a successful roll, would put him three shots ahead with just two holes left. He drained it—one of the most pressure-filled putts of his life. And in that moment, it was clear: Rory McIlroy was on the verge of history.

The 18th hole arrived, and McIlroy, with a three-shot lead, walked down the final fairway to a standing ovation. His approach shot to the green was flawless, landing within 10 feet of the pin. As he sank the final putt, the roar from the patrons echoed throughout Augusta National. He had done it. After years of near misses, after countless heartbreaks, Rory McIlroy had finally won the Masters.

The Green Jacket, Finally

When McIlroy slipped on the green jacket later that evening, it wasn't just the culmination of a tournament. It was the culmination of a career, a personal odyssey, and a moment he would cherish for the rest of his life. The Sunday at the 2025 Masters was not just a win—it was a statement. Rory McIlroy had triumphed, and in doing so, had cemented his place as one of golf's all-time greats.

CONCLUSION

Beyond the Grand Slam

Rory McIlroy's victory at the 2025 Masters Tournament was not just another addition to his already impressive resume. It was the final, golden piece in a puzzle that had taken years to complete. The Grand Slam—an achievement that had eluded him for over a decade—was no longer a distant dream. It was a reality, one that only six men before him had ever known. And yet, as McIlroy stood on the 18th green at Augusta, holding the coveted green jacket, the true significance of his achievement was not just in the historical context but in what it represented for him personally and for the sport of golf.

McIlroy's win at Augusta marked the end of a long and often painful pursuit. For years, the elusive green jacket had hung just out of his reach, tantalizingly close yet always slipping away. The ghosts of past Masters, where McIlroy had led or been in contention but ultimately faltered, were a constant reminder of the challenges Augusta posed for him. There were times when those failures threatened to define his career. But on this

Sunday, at the age of 35, McIlroy proved to the world—and to himself—that he was more than his struggles. He was a champion, one of the greatest to ever play the game.

The Significance of the Masters Victory

The Masters has always held a special place in the hearts of golfers and fans alike. It is steeped in tradition, history, and prestige. Winning it is considered the pinnacle of success in the sport. The green jacket is more than just a trophy; it is a symbol of mastery, of the ability to overcome the unique challenges that Augusta National presents. For McIlroy, it was the final piece of the modern Grand Slam puzzle, an achievement that only a select few have managed to attain.

The victory was also significant because of the context in which it occurred. McIlroy's journey to Augusta in 2025 had been marked by consistency, resilience, and a deeper understanding of his own game. His win at the Masters was not just a flash of brilliance but the result of years of hard work, refinement, and growth. It was the culmination of a career that had already seen him win multiple majors, dominate the PGA Tour, and reach the summit of the World Golf Rankings. But it was also the answer to the lingering question that had followed him for over a decade: Could McIlroy win at Augusta?

By conquering the Masters, McIlroy did more than just add a major title to his name. He removed the stigma of being a player who could not win at Augusta, a label that had unfairly stuck to him despite his undeniable talent. The Masters was the one major that seemed to be just out of his reach, and in 2025, he exorcised that demon.

The Personal Journey

McIlroy's victory at the Masters was as much about personal growth as it was about golf. The struggles he faced over the years were not only about his golf game but about his evolution as a person. He had dealt with public scrutiny, personal challenges, and periods of self-doubt. But through it all, McIlroy never wavered from his commitment to his craft. His win at Augusta was a testament to his mental fortitude, his ability to learn from his mistakes, and his unwavering belief in himself.

Throughout his career, McIlroy had spoken openly about his mental and emotional struggles. The pressure of being one of the most talented golfers of his generation came with its own set of challenges. There were times when the weight of expectations seemed unbearable, when the desire to prove himself overshadowed the joy of playing. But as he matured, McIlroy found peace in his approach to the game. His victory at Augusta was not just about conquering the course or the field; it was about conquering himself. It was about letting go of the past and embracing the present, knowing that he was more than capable of achieving greatness.

A Career Rewritten

The 2025 Masters was the final act in McIlroy's journey to a career Grand Slam. With his win at Augusta, he joined an elite group of players, including Jack Nicklaus, Tiger Woods, Ben Hogan, Gary Player, and Gene Sarazen, who had completed the set of major victories. For McIlroy, this victory redefined his legacy. No longer would he be remembered solely for his early promise and near misses. Instead, he would be remembered as one of the most complete golfers to ever play the game—a man who overcame adversity, learned from his setbacks, and triumphed on the biggest stage in golf.

The achievement also allowed McIlroy to shift the narrative of his career. Before Augusta, there were whispers about whether McIlroy would ever achieve the career Grand Slam. There were questions about his ability to perform in the pressure cooker that is the Masters. But with that green jacket, McIlroy silenced those doubts once and for all. He had completed what many thought was impossible for him, cementing his place in history.

Golf's New Era: The End of an Era?

McIlroy's victory at Augusta marked the closing of a chapter in the sport of golf. With Tiger Woods' era gradually fading due to injury and age, McIlroy was positioned to take the mantle as the face of modern golf. His win at the Masters, combined with his consistency on the PGA Tour and his broad appeal, solidified his place at the top of the game.

But McIlroy's victory also represented the beginning of a new era in golf. With his career Grand Slam in hand, McIlroy was now a bridge between two generations of golfers. He was part of the last generation to experience the Woods-dominated era while also ushering in the next generation of stars like Scottie Scheffler, Collin Morikawa, and Viktor Hovland. McIlroy had proven that a new champion had emerged, one who could carry the sport forward and inspire the next wave of golfers.

Looking Forward: A New Horizon

As McIlroy walked off the 18th green at Augusta, he knew that his journey was far from over. The Masters was the culmination of one chapter, but it opened the door to many more. The victory had solidified his place in history, but there was still plenty more to achieve. His career Grand Slam was a testament to his resilience and his ability to adapt to the ever-changing demands of the game. But there was still the pursuit of more titles, more wins, and the chance to inspire future generations of golfers.

The 2025 Masters also marked the start of a new phase in McIlroy's life. The victory had come at a time when he was in a mature phase of his career, having already achieved so much and with a sense of fulfillment. What lay ahead was not just about adding more trophies to his cabinet, but about leaving a legacy that transcended the golf course. McIlroy's influence on the sport, his advocacy for mental health, and his ability to connect with fans of all ages were as important as his achievements on the course.

In the end, McIlroy's victory at the Masters wasn't just about winning one tournament. It was about the journey—the highs, the lows, the perseverance, and the evolution of a man who had become the complete golfer. As he left the 18th green, with the green jacket draped over his shoulders, Rory McIlroy had achieved something far greater than the Grand Slam. He had achieved greatness on his own terms. And that, more than anything, was the true reward.

Printed in Dunstable, United Kingdom

73827273R00037